The Pursuit of Transformation

How to Take Action

Accompanies *The Pursuit of More*
&
The Pursuit of Forgiveness 2.0

**The Pursuit of Transformation
How to Take Action**

ISBN: 978-1-7327804-6-0
Copyright © 2020
By Melissa Reese, The Pursuit Guru

All rights reserved. No part of this book may be reproduced or distributed in any form, except for the inclusion of brief quotations in review, without permission in writing from the author.

Printed in the United States.

Edited by Melinda Splitek

Thank you to all the people that have supported my work. Thank you to all the clients that have helped me learn and grow as a practitioner and as a person. Thank you to all the pioneers, gurus, teachers, visionaries, and life students that encourage and broadcast self-help, self-development, quantum physics, epigenetic science, heart and neuroscience, herbalism, and energetic healing.

Thank you to my husband, my mom, my dad, my brother, my sister/cuz, my dearest friends (you know who you are), and family (both biological and chosen).
I am one fortunate being.

It is my intention to share and encourage LOVE, knowledge, and wisdom with all that are seeking to embrace more joy, happiness, peace, and fulfillment.

Preface

Knowledge has no power unless it is actually utilized. You only become empowered when you apply what you know in the ways that work best for you. Reading and learning new information is fantastic. This helps you become more knowledgeable. Next, you need to implement the acquired knowledge; this is where wisdom is born and how you truly experience clarity and empowerment. Take a wise approach to your healing and transformative journey. This guide is designed to help you navigate this journey.

After, or even while, reading *The Pursuit of More* and *The Pursuit of Forgiveness 2.0*, take time to sit with yourself and dig into the questions presented throughout this workbook. I encourage you to use a journal or legal pad to respond to the questions so that you have enough room for your answers and the opportunity to do this again in the future and compare your new answers to your previous ones. Refer back to the books and anything you highlighted. This is your opportunity to learn more about yourself, get to know yourself better, and to understand yourself. This is your opportunity to let go of the false self, the illusionary self, and to heal, grow, evolve, change, transform, and LOVE yourself.

If you are unaware of a problem, how do you solve it? By answering the questions in this workbook, you are becoming more aware. With awareness comes opportunity and responsibility - an opportunity to grow and a responsibility to yourself to do the necessary work. Once you have more awareness, then you can do something with it and about it. This workbook, along with my other books and recordings, are meant to help you navigate your new awareness and to heal. This workbook is your opportunity to start, or to continue, doing the essential work within yourself so that you may experience the life you want and need.

This workbook guides you through a reflective process that relates to your perception of yourself, presently and in the future. It also poses reflective questions related to self-care/self-LOVE, relationships, mental and emotional health, spirituality, and pursuits and goals. At the end of each section, I include a short list of resources for you that relate to the topic. At the end, there is a full list of resources for you to engage with as you feel called.

I also recommend downloading the following recordings from my website: "The Forgiveness Processes", "Forgetting to Remembering Meditation", and "The Pendulum Meditation."

My website is www.thepursuitguru.com.

Take your time with this work. Go at your own pace. Be intentional. There is no rush to any finish line, it's about the journey itself. This is the work of your life, for your life. Life is ever evolving – sometimes, it's a lot at once and sometimes, it seems stagnant. Be true to you - do the work you feel you need to and do it in the ways that work best for you. This is not a time for judgement. It is a time for observing with LOVE.

A Note to Journeyers

If you are dealing with serious and deep trauma that results in panic attacks or other serious reactions, have been labeled with PTSD, or some other psychological label; in addition to this workbook, please seek help from a professional. In-person or live internet sessions with a professional are highly recommended. I recommend finding a practitioner with multiple modalities that include such practices as NLP (Neuro-Linguistic Programming) and Hypnotherapy. These are efficient and effective ways to heal and overcome trauma in a short amount of time. I also recommend finding a good Naturopathic doctor or Functional Medical doctor, as most psychological issues are due to past experiences and are greatly worsened by diet, gut health, and environment.

This workbook will help you, and it's going to bring your "stuff" to the surface. The books I have written and the recordings I've done are all filled with information on how to strengthen your abilities and empower yourself to be more courageous so that you may overcome the fears, hurts, angers, and pains that seem to plague and stifle you. Even with all this information, you may not have all the tools to completely work through or overcome this "stuff" on your own; you may need some help from a practitioner to fully process and heal the "stuff." Please seek out a practitioner you feel comfortable with to do the necessary work. Should you want to work with me, I have one-to-one appointments available and can be contacted via my website.

You are meant to heal. You are equipped with all you need to heal—you just need to learn how to readily access it, familiarize yourself with it, and learn how to make it a habit in your life. It all starts with the unwavering decision to create change in your own life for the sake of your well-being.

Change does not have to be complicated or take a long time. Life never has to be about desperation; learn how to navigate before it gets to that point. Shift into a life created from a space of soul, peace, love, and inspiration. Your life, your way.

An Explanation of Terms

Perception: This refers to your unique views and ideologies of your life, others' lives, and the world around you; your personal internalized reality based on your current interpretation of known information. Perception can be ever changing as it is based upon all of our experiences, beliefs, culture, abilities, practices, health, level of understanding, and values until now. When any one of those things changes, shifts, or transforms, so does your perception.

Aligned: When you are aligned, your soul, spirit, and ego all communicate easily and effortlessly allowing you to know when anything is good, bad, right, wrong, somewhere in between, or even unclear. You know when you need more information or time, and you know when you are decided. You listen to and know you can trust and follow your intuition void of doubt.

Congruent: When you are congruent, you say what you mean and mean what you say. What you do and how you do it stems from your integrity and values. You unwaveringly abide by and trust your life's compass and calibrate accordingly. You only engage with what is 'right' and true for you.

Mind: Your mind is comprised of your brain, heart, gut, and entire body. The mind is both within you and outside of you. The mind is the seat of all of our thoughts, imagination, creations, memories, behaviors, and how you experience all of life. It is influenced by energy, diet, beliefs, experiences, information, cellular health, and environment. The mind influences your ego, and your ego influences it.

Ego: The Ego refers to the unique "self" individualized from the rest of the world and others. It is influenced by emotions, experiences, relationships, and beliefs - the external experience internalized, as it relates to you. Your feeling of "self" expressed internally and projected externally. The Ego is influenced by the mind and the mind influences the Ego.

Malnourished Ego: Consider this an ego fed with Twinkies and the like. A malnourished ego needs to hear praise from others over and over, for without that praise, the "self" feels deflated, agitated, and/or worthless. A malnourished ego insults, dehumanizes, degrades, and lacks in praising others, and overpraises the "self." A malnourished ego focuses on "self" in ways that is void of recognizing the needs and wants of anyone else. It has a difficult time with, or fails to see the strength, beauty, wonderful attributes, and value of others. It operates from a place of lack and engages exclusivity. A malnourished ego is preoccupied by and/or fixated on competition and winning; fragile.

Nourished or Light Ego: Consider this an ego fed with kale and the like. A nourished or light ego praises others and "self" with joy, gratitude, respect, and LOVE. A nourished or light ego sees its unique gifts and recognizes others unique gifts and talents. It builds both the *self* and others up; thus allowing an inclusive and greater experience of happiness and being nurtured. A nourished or light ego knows all abundance and gratitude and engages inclusivity. It knows the importance of practicing self-care and self-love for the greater good and encourages others to do the same. A nourished or light ego is very comfortable with the "self", unshaken by other's opinions and also willing to listen; not Fragile.

True Self/Soul: This refers to your very nature; your unique essence; your genius. This is who you are, void of all the influence you've encountered since conception. The True Self/Soul is your purest, uninfluenced "self" that is fully aligned - your soul, body, and spirit recognized and expressed. When expressed in its entirety, it helps keep your ego nourished. When you die, it transforms from being your specific identity and fully unites with Sprit Energy into the Collective Energy/LOVE.

Your Spirit: Your Sprit is your higher self. The connective energy that simultaneously embodies you and the Collective Energy. Your Spirit is the energy that knows all and is forever continuous; the energy within you that connects you to the Divine, Creation, God, Allah, Yahweh, Life Force, Life Source, Energy, Spirit, Universe, or whatever you call the 'greater than.'

This energy never dies; it simply transitions from being a connecting energy to fully uniting with the Collective Energy.

LOVE: LOVE refers to a space, place, domain, experience, feeling, all knowing, truth, connection, total peace, void of judgement and separation or separatism, yummy energy.

Introduction

Your mind is the most powerful tool you possess. Your mind is comprised of physical attributes and energetic attributes. The mind relies on the physical health of your gut, heart, and brain. It also relies on your energetic, emotional, mental, and spiritual health to function optimally. In order for your mind to be healthy and strong, you must nourish and nurture multiple levels of yourself. This means that what you eat, watch, listen to, think about, feel, and do, all matter so much. What habits do you have that are benefitting your utmost well-being? What habits do you have that contribute to your least favorite aspects about yourself and the world around you?

Being the best version of you takes willingness, determination, effort, and active participation in knowing your truest self and healing all that keeps you from experiencing that version of you. The best version of you feels fulfilled, happy, joyful, content, at peace, and in LOVE with every aspect of who you are and how you show up each and every day - knowing that you are a perpetual work in progress and making progress daily. Are you willing to dig into all of who you are, all that makes up *you*? Are you willing to learn how to LOVE every aspect of yourself and forgive the less than perfect aspects in order to shift, transform, and let go of detrimental internalizations of self?

There is the ego part of self, the soul part of self (true self), and the spirit part of self. These parts make up the internalized whole of you. These combined are what make you human, and it is imperative that you nourish and nurture them. If one is malnourished, you are out of alignment, imbalanced, conflicted, disassociated, disillusioned, disheartened, disoriented, and living a life that feels or seems void of purpose, meaning, and fulfillment.

Ego is a human trait; without it we would no longer be human. Your soul is the very embodiment that makes you uniquely you. Your spirit is the energy that never dies and is your connection to whatever you recognize as that greater energy, creation, and LOVE.

It's good to have a nourished and enriched ego, and it's good to be so connected to your soul that you are able to hear it, acknowledge it, and embody it in all you think, believe, and do. It's also imperative to have some sort of spiritual or connective practice such as being in and with nature, meditation, prayer, and anything that focuses on a loving, connecting energy greater than just you. By having a relationship with Light or Life Energy you are better able to recharge, feel rejuvenated, practice presence, and grow your awareness. The wisest people have some sort of loving or spiritual connection practice.

> *Note: Intelligence and wisdom are not necessarily the same things. All that are wise have great intelligence, but not all that are intelligent are wise. Wisdom determines how you utilize the intelligence that you have. Your intelligence can create or destroy, encourage movement or promote stagnancy, have you experience happiness or misery based on how wise you are.*

Questions to Briefly Consider

Do you have a malnourished or nourished ego? Do you know which one you most operate from? Which one are you letting define you? Do you have a malnourished or nourished soul? Are you denying your soul? And are you in communication with your spirit (higher self)? Are you wisely utilizing your intelligence? As you dig in you will be able to answer these questions with confidence.

Digging into YOU

Are you willing to dig into all of who you are, all of that which makes up you? Are you willing to learn how to LOVE every aspect of yourself and forgive the less than perfect aspects in order to shift, transform, and let go of detrimental internalizations of self?

We are molded by our family, environment, friends, religion, schools, culture, experiences, food, and more. This is how we form beliefs, values, characteristics, behaviors, emotions, and overall health experience. We inherit and take on so much from others when we are young that it's hard to differentiate what actually belongs to our deepest and truest self and what we've taken on and identified with from others - having woven it into who we know ourselves to be. We have to unravel what we think we know so that we can better understand what is actually true for ourselves as unique individuals.

We can keep what serves us in wonderful ways and we can unlearn what we've previously been taught or programmed to believe that is a disservice to us and potentially harmful. Many people live life making one unconscious decision after another and journey further down the path to feeling more unfulfilled, more unhappy, more stuck, or more lost. To live consciously and conscientiously for your well-being is to live within awareness and to be present.

To become aware, dig in, and better understand is a process and one that continues throughout our life as we learn, grow, and evolve. The awareness of our 'stuff' versus others' 'stuff' is the first place to start. We must take responsibility for ourselves and continue to be responsible to ourselves, and for ourselves.

Befriend yourself. When befriending someone you ask them about their wishes, desires, dreams, goals, likes, dislikes, favorites, people in their life, and so much more. Think about the things you do for best friends; the ways in which you show up and support them. Do this with yourself. Become your own best friend.

Nourished beliefs, nourished behaviors, and nurtured presence are all you need to live your best life for your utmost well-being. When you believe differently, you do differently. The only person that can implement and practice these things is you for the sake of you. All that you need to get started is within and around you. It's time to dig in. Dig in with curiosity, healthy skepticism, openness, willingness, and determination.

Bonus Process

Utilize this along with the other processes in *The Pursuit of More*.

> **Light Process:** *Here is method to use along with the breathing technique to start to eliminate some baggage with LOVE and Light.*
>
> *Sit with yourself, breathe, and notice where you are experiencing discomfort, stress, mental/emotional 'pain,' etc. Identify the characteristics of what you're experiencing, i.e., color, texture, weight, etc.*
>
> *Use loving, healing white light to encapsulate things within you that you want to get rid of, be free from, release. Wrap the light around it and imagine pulling it from your body. Say what you need to it, if you need to, then dissolve it with LOVE and Light and let a vacuum of Love/light suck it all up. Make sure to fill that space in your body back up with gratitude, LOVE, anything positive and the loving, healing light.*

As You Are Now

Use the Breathing Technique as described in my books and found on my YouTube channel, The Pursuit Guru. Be with yourself now, in a space void of distractions. Allow your focus to be inward as you give yourself permission to answer the following questions fully and honestly.

As you reflect on yourself, what emotions and feelings do you experience the most in your life on a daily basis? (i.e., happiness, fear, joy, envy, hopeful, fret, gratitude, anger, grief, sadness, hurt, excitement, love, etc.)

Questions for Reflection

Who do you see yourself as?

> *Be as honest as you are able to. Your ability to acknowledge all your varying attributes is what places you in the pilot seat of your vessel and better able to navigate your life more effectively and authentically.*

List your characteristics, ideas, and defining qualities about who you think you are and how you see yourself.

> *Example: I see myself as a person that is respectful of 'x', loves to share 'x', is open minded, sometimes defensive, sensitive, bold, courageous, and fearful all at the same time... I see myself as a leader. I see myself as a someone that cares deeply about 'x' and does my best to contribute in the following ways... I see myself as a big work in progress... I see myself as likable... I see myself as lazy and unmotivated... I see myself as someone that is athletic, but needs more work to look how I idealize myself to look...*

What are your best attributes, not that have been told to you by others, but that you feel are really true about you? (non-physical and physical)

What do you deem right?

What do you deem wrong?

What do you believe to be good?

What do you believe to be bad?

From all that you just listed as right, wrong, good, bad, do those things apply just for you or for others as well? Meaning, you adhere to and abide by those things for yourself and don't necessarily expect others to do the same.

Do you do you also expect others to adhere to and abide by what you have categorized as right, wrong, good, bad?

How do you feel when you slack on abiding by these categorizations?

How do you feel when others do not adhere to or abide by these categorizations?

When do you find yourself most resistant?

What are you most resistant to?

What do you feel you are resisting?

What is the resistance about?

> *What you resist persists. Have a conversation with the resistance. Is there resistance to do something, think something, believe something, create something, try something, etc.? Resistance is not hesitance; they are very different. Hesitancy is about being on the fence and needing to check in with yourself on how this thing or person needs to be handled, not whether you handled it at all. Resistance comes from deep within and is typically the shadow of your soul's essence (your genius). Your essence/genius wants to express itself and fear is doing its best to divert and steal your attention by expressing itself emphatically and with more desperation.*

How much do you focus on how others live their lives?

How much do you focus on how you live your life?

What aspects (from your lists above) would you say are your ego self? Which would you say are nourished? Which could use some nourishment?

What aspects (from your lists above) would you say are your true self, your soul?

How do you think others see you? What have others told you about you?

What do you believe to be deeply true about what you think about yourself?

What do you believe to be deeply true about what others think about you?

How do you talk to yourself?

What do you say?

How much is positive and how much is negative?

Do you think you operate from your true self with a nourished ego or your constructed self with either a slightly, moderate, or significantly malnourished ego self most often?

Which self would you say more defines how you show up in the world? Do you feel that your ego self (whatever condition it's in) and true self are aligned?

> *You can be doing what you LOVE, operating from your soul's essence, your genius if you will, and you can still have and out-of-whack-ego. If you feel you are acting, putting on a show, putting on a "good face", withholding or holding back, feeling better than others, feeling less than others, needing to compete more often than not, are one way with some people or groups and are another way with other people and groups, you are essentially acting inauthentically. These behaviors are connected to your malnourished ego; this is your false self - an illusion.*

When do you feel most yourself? (with people and in situations - list it all)

Who is currently in your life? (close friends, periphery friends, acquaintances, co-workers, family, etc.)

Do the people you've listed uplift, nourish, encourage, respect, and fully accept you as you are? Or do they frustrate, deplete, disrespect, insult, make suggestion on who or what you should be, and/or what you should be doing?

> *People can be multiple things in your life, use the words above and any other words to describe that person in your relationship with them.*

What people and things have played a big role in your life (in the past)?

What people and things currently play a big role in your life (now)?

Who are some people and/or groups that you actively avoid in your life?

What are some things that you actively avoid in your life?

Is there anyone or anything else, now that you're thinking about it, that you avoid and didn't really realize it until just now?

What habits do you have that are benefitting your utmost well-being?

What habits do you have that contribute to your least favorite aspects about yourself and the world around you?

Say you received 12 compliments and/or glowing reviews, 2 middle of the road compliments and/or glowing reviews, and one "scathing" insult and/or review. What do you tend to focus on? What do you give your energy to? How does this influence how you feel about yourself, think about yourself, and talk to yourself?

What are you worthy of?

What are you deserving of?

Who or what are you allowing to determine your self-worth?

Where do you feel you need more grace in your life?

How can you give yourself and others more grace?*

*For more info on grace, see the chapter on grace in The Pursuit of Forgiveness 2.0.

As Your Best Self

Use the Breathing Technique again now and allow yourself to shift into a different space. Imagine that you could invite in the happiest, most joyful, most fulfilled, brightest, fullest, most LOVING, most true version of yourself. Engage with this version of yourself—see, hear, feel, and experience this version of you.

> At the end of the workbook, once you've completely dug in and done some transformative work, you will have the opportunity to describe your most ideal self and life. This description will be more in-depth and more dynamic than what you will come up with here. For now, just do this part of the workbook to the best of your ability. This is

how you start to really engage your soul, spirit, and imagination. This will allow your mind and sense of self to be expressed in an evolutionary manner. I invite you to compare what you write here, to what you write when you've completed your journey through this workbook.

Who do you want to be? How do you truly want to see yourself mentally, emotionally, physically, and spiritually?

What do you deem right, wrong, good, or bad for yourself?

What are the characteristics of your best self?

What do you want your best life to look like?

What do you want your best life to feel like?

What are you worthy of?

What are you deserving of?

Who and what gets to determine your self-worth?

What does your best self believe? (about yourself, others, the world around you, spirituality, your past, your present, and your future)

Who would be in your life? (close friends, periphery friends, acquaintances, co-workers, family, etc.)

What type of people do you want to surround yourself with? What do these people "bring out" from within you?

What things do you actively and intentionally engage in your life?

What habits do you have that are benefitting your utmost well-being?

Say you received 12 compliments and/or glowing reviews, two middle of the road compliments and/or glowing reviews, and one "scathing" insult and/or review. What do you tend to focus on? What do you give your energy to? How does this influence how you feel about yourself, think about yourself, and talk to yourself?

Reflect on your answers. Where does there seem to be blocks mentally, emotionally, and physically. Where in your body do you experience aches, pains, discomfort, more energy, less energy, and anything else you can pinpoint and describe?

Start with pursuing one thing to transform and change—when you feel a shift and feel like you are ready to keep going, do so. This is all about your journey. This is not a quick dash to the finish line. Take one step, do one thing, engage a willingness, be patient, be determined, and make the essential efforts for forward movement, as small or as big as you are able to do for any given day. Rejoice when you have an epiphany, gain understanding, learn something new, set aside time for just you, experience any shift, transformation, or change.

You get to decide where you really need to start. Start with utilizing the Bonus Process near the beginning of the workbook, the processes listed in the back of *The Pursuit of More*, and the Forgiveness Process recordings. I also have guided meditations available on www.thepursuitguru.com. The processes take practice, but stick with it, and grant yourself patience and grace.

Suggested Resources

The Biology of Belief by Bruce Lipton

You are the Placebo by Dr. Joe Dispenza

The Anatomy of A Calling by Lissa Rankin

The Four Agreements by Don Miguel Ruiz

The Five Levels of Attachment by Don Miguel Ruiz Jr.

What the Bleep Do We Know - documentary

Self-Care, Self-LOVE

Self-LOVE and self-care are not about being self-involved. It does not mean that you are solely focused on the "self" above anything else. This is not about narcissism. This is not about being self-centered. It is not always about putting yourself first. You put yourself first when you feel you are depleted or diminished in some way. You put yourself first when there is something you need to work through. It is solely about answering to your soul, body, and mind.

Self-LOVE and self-care are about aligning your soul, spirit, and nourished ego. It is about being clear and concise with your words and actions, for the sake of yourself and others. This work is about knowing yourself so truly and deeply and caring for yourself accordingly. It is about nourishing yourself, nurturing yourself, and continuing to do the essential work to check in with yourself so that you can be the best you. You have a responsibility to show up for yourself; you have the responsibility to show up in this world as someone who encourages others to do the same. You nourish, nurture, and strengthen yourself and then share that strength and best version of self with those that you choose. All this work is what allows you to better share your essence, your genius, your soul with the world in the ways that feel the best for you. You are meant to share you with the world; however, you feel called to do so.

Self-Care is all about but not limited to: massages, eating a clean diet, staying hydrated, nourishing your mind, nourishing your soul, reading, spending time in nature, a standing appointment with a life coach or other practitioner, traveling, mindful gratitude, learning, being with loved ones, staring a blank wall, gazing at the stars, a retreat, "mani's" and "pedi's," exercising, meditating, saying yes when you mean yes, saying no when you mean no, knowing why you are saying yes and no, knowing whom you are saying yes or no for, accepting compliments, loving who you are at the deepest level, working through and healing your fears, hurts, pains, injustices, resentments, plain old' shit, and forgiveness. It is also, anything that creates joy, happiness, LOVE, nourishes you, nurtures you, helps with you experiencing more calm and peace in your being and life, encourages growth, awareness, presence, and well-being.

Questions for Reflection

What do you enjoy?

What brings you joy, happiness, and feelings of fulfillment?

What do you find relaxing?

What do you actually do to relax and unwind?

How often do you relax and unwind?

Of the things you do to relax and unwind, which are nourishing and nurturing and which might merely be distractions or just other forms of mind and energy preoccupation?

Do you think it's important to take uninterrupted time for yourself?

Do you believe you have to earn your relaxation time?

Are you deserving of time - time to yourself to relax and unwind?

Are you able to sit in silence - meaning by yourself with no music, TV, or conversation?

> *Being out in nature with natural animal and water sounds is different.*

If so, for how long are you able to be in silence, with yourself, until you need some noise or distraction?

If not, what seems so difficult or uncomfortable about being in silence with yourself?

What do you do out of a sense of obedience or obligation rather than pure choice?

> *Obedience is often, although not always, a restrictive thing. Obligation is what you said yes to that has you experiencing feeling stuck, handcuffed, shackled, indebted, and without choice. Obligation and commitment are not the same. Obligations are 'have to's', 'musts', 'shoulds', placed on you by others that you accept because you feel like you can't say no, you have no choice, and/or you feel pressured. Obligations typically only serve and/or benefit one party involved. Commitments are something you happily enter into and do because they feel good and are mutually beneficial for all parties involved. Commitments never feel manipulative, heavy, dreaded, or the like. Commitments can turn to obligation when dynamics shift, and then you must recalibrate if you are able to. The intention is to lose the obligations and keep the commitments in your life.*

What is your diet like? Be sure to consider what you eat, watch, listen to, do, and who you surround yourself with most often.

Is this diet working well for you?

> *Reflect on previous experiences (and keep this in mind for any future experiences). Notice your mood after you eat. Are you happy, angry/irritable, energized, sluggish, etc.? Notice your mood when you are with certain people or after you leave being around certain people. Notice which activities drain you or energize you.*

What about your diet needs to change for you to feel healthier, more energetic, more joyful, and more nourished?

What can you do to care more for your "self" and your over-all well-being? What do you need to add in? What do you need to remove?

Are you good at asking for help?

Are you good at accepting help when receiving help?

Are you getting help from people and things that are actually helpful?

Do you know where to go and who to ask for the help you most need/desire?

What are your 'non-negotiables'? (Meaning what you protect at all costs—that others are never allowed to infiltrate, upset, negotiate, manipulate, or take.)

Example: Your inner peace could be non-negotiable. Other examples might include your happiness, joy, mental freedom, emotional freedom, your health, and well-being, and/or your practices: meditation, prayer, exercise, etc. The things you choose are what are sacred, precious, and absolutely necessary for you. You do the work, set the boundaries, and make damn sure that you are the one calling the shots to maintain, nourish, and nurture your non-negotiables.

If you do not have any 'non-negotiables', what would be the most important for you to implement?

How would you implement them? What would it take?

What and who do you need to forgive and possibly let go of?

If you feel as though you are struggling, I invite you to search for people that have seemingly found more flow in their lives and find out how they accomplished that, only apply what you feel called to. Find platforms that seem to help others do this as well – again, only engage with what calls to you. In the back of the workbook, I have provided a comprehensive list of people and organizations on social media that I believe post helpful and beneficial information. I have also provided you with other books, videos, and platforms that provide nourishing and nurturing information for any help and transformation you seek. Engage with what calls to you.

Suggested Resources

The Mastery of Love by Don Miguel Ruiz

Big Magic by Elizabeth Gilbert

Love, Medicine, & Miracles by Bernie Siegel, MD

Mind Over Medicine by Lissa Rankin

The Honeymoon Effect by Bruce Lipton

The Cure Is - documentary

Relationships

There are many types of relationships: romantic, familial, friends, business, spiritual, food, money, homes, and cars, and more.

Questions for Reflection

What relationships in your life seem to be the most difficult or strained?

What relationships seem to need the most attention and work in your life? Is the attention and work you put in out of commitment or obligation?

What relationships do you have that you would like to be free from? Remember to consider those that are toxic, unhealthy, frustrating, unsteady, draining, lackluster, old, too infrequent, etc.

What type of relationships do you want? Remember to describe the category of relationship along with characteristics and values of the relationship you desire/want/need.

What is the purpose of or for the relationships you want?

What would they bring to your life? Consider why are they important and what's driving the want/need for these relationships as well.

Why a particular person and/or thing? What about them draws you in and holds meaning?

What action are you willing to take to create the relationships that you've named?

How will you nurture and nourish each of your unique relationships?

Do you believe you are worthy and deserving of a relationship in which you are respected and honored?

What does being respected and honored in any relationship mean to you? (for any relationship)

How is your relationship with yourself?

How do you talk to yourself, think about yourself, treat yourself with eating, going out, exercising, TV (both duration of time with it and what you choose to watch), etc.?

How could your relationship with yourself be more nurtured and nourished?

Who do you need a break from? Who do you need to LOVE from afar? **This break can be as long as you need it to be.*

Who or what do you need to forgive?

Your relationship with yourself is very telling. It will unveil, teach you, and help you to understand all the other relationships you keep in your life. You must start with you first. Take a look at how you answered the questions about relationships with others and things and see what that may tell you about yourself. Now take a look at how you answered the questions about your relationship with yourself and see what that tells you about your other relationships. Grace, respect, commitment, reverence, healthy boundaries, communication, and LOVE are the very most important things in any relationship, especially the one with yourself.

If you notice that you are not feeling worthy and deserving of respect and honor or haven't really given deep thought into what that looks like and means to you, please spend some time with this. Did someone in your past tell you that you are undeserving or unworthy? Did you somehow internalize being unworthy or undeserving based on something you heard, learned, or experienced? Work on forgiving yourself as well as the person, institution, and experience that helped create this narrative.

Remember that what you value in a relationship is not necessarily what someone else values in a relationship, some refer to these attributes as love language. It's also just how you internalize ideas, concepts, and experiences.* In your relationships, make sure you communicate and have a conversation about your values and needs. Efforts need to be made by each party involved to do their best to respect, practice, and appreciate varying values and needs or the relationship will break down.

If you have a relationship with a thing, not a person, the success and fulfillment of that relationship is a direct reflection of you, you can only calibrate you in this situation. Example of 'things': money, food, vehicle, home, building, church, school, sports, sports team, clothing, sex, etc. Your level of attachment to something determines your feelings for it and how healthy your relationship is to it.

*See The Pursuit of Forgiveness 2.0, page 27 for an example.

Suggested Resources

The Honeymoon Effect by Bruce Lipton

The Untethered Soul by Michael A. Singer

The Mastery of Self by Don Miguel Ruiz Jr.

The Fifth Agreement by Don Miguel Ruiz

Braving the Wilderness by Brene Brown

Mental and Emotional Health

Your mental health, emotional health, and overall well-being create a somewhat delicate ecosystem that can change in an instant. Sometimes this instant has such an impact, it influences your entire ecosystem, and other times, it is just momentary. Your level of self-care directly and significantly impacts your ecosystem. You've already listed the people in your life and those you'd like to shift out of your life. You've also become aware of your joys, passions, sorrows, and pains. Your emotions, your thoughts, your beliefs, your activities, your food diet, your information-intake diet, and the environment around you all influence your ecosystem. Some things have a greater impact than others.

As you reflect on the work you've already done above, take a look at any patterns you see. From the type of people that are in your life to your interests in food, music, entertainment, energy levels, moods, etc. Do you see any patterns? Is there a message for you in what you've already uncovered? What impacts your ecosystem the most? These things determine how healthy you are in terms of your mental and emotional health. They also determine how nourishing or detrimental they are to your well-being. You have to nurture your ecosystem by nourishing it with books, videos, music, entertainment, conversations, food, and environments that promote good health, learning, growth, well-being, dynamic awareness, and self-development. These things will be unique to you and may look similar to what others engage with, but always make sure that what you invite in is in alignment with your true self, your soul. This is how you maintain your ecosystem, feel more fulfilled, and keep your entire being healthier.

Your emotions are not bigger than you. They are not what control you unless you allow them to. When our emotions control us, they dictate our entire well-being, our decisions, our outcomes, and our entire life. When you know how to harness and navigate your emotions you live a healthier, happier, more fulfilled life. Just as you want to be heard and others want to be heard, our emotions want to be heard. So, it is our duty to converse with them and get to know them intimately. This is to know our "self" intimately, deeply, and fully. This is how we are able to experience our emotions in all their dynamic, healthy, and full expression. This is how we are best able to navigate, deal with, and get through anything we need to. Remember to reflect from a place of observation free of judgement.

Questions for Reflection

What triggers you in a negative way? (What upsets you, gets you frustrated or flustered easily?)

> *Notice the times when you feel a rise of agitation, frustration, anger, unease, discomfort - just notice and observe; avoid trying to figure out why. Ask yourself, "What is this about?" Or "What about this upsets me?"*

> *These are not triggers that may come from a "gut" feeling about something feeling off or wrong; this is about pinpointing reactions from an already 'pressed button'. When we are negatively triggered, or rapidly become upset, it often comes from a place of past, irrational, and/or constructed fear and not rational or primal fear. From fear also comes judgement, and judgement is typically present in a negative triggered state and/or reactionary response.*

> *If you ask, "Why am I feeling/experiencing this?", you will only get excuses and reasons that are mostly not sound due to the state you are in. No one else created the state you are in; you did that from within you. Your reaction is based on your belief system, values, and your perception of your world and the world around you. You are the one that has trained yourself how to react and respond; you either allowed others to encourage and influence that or not. This is why it's not a matter of why, but how or what. How did you get 'there'? How did you get to where you're at? What did you accept at any level as true?*

All of our behaviors are based upon our beliefs. As our beliefs change, our behaviors change.

What behaviors would you like to transform?

What beliefs do you hold that drive the behavior that you'd like to transform?

> *Example: If you dislike the fact that you are a smoker and would like to become a nonsmoker, but have a really hard time changing the behavior, think about what drives you to smoke. How do you know it's time to have a cigarette? Do you really believe that cigarettes are bad? Do you feel on some level you are not worthy of being healthy? Do you believe it's too difficult to be healthy? Do you maybe have some beliefs around death? See how beliefs influence our behaviors? It can be conscious or at a subconscious level. It's our job to dig in and find the beliefs that cause us to continue to choose the wrong partner, friends, foods, etc. I've worked with people that at a deep subconscious level believed they deserved to be tortured or punished, so they naively continued to choose things and people in life that fulfilled this belief. It's hard to always know where a belief comes from, and it really doesn't matter, all that matters is you acknowledge that it resides within you and then you do something about it.*
>
> *You might dislike that you are "promiscuous" or a "serial monogamist." You might dislike that you have issues with food. You might dislike that you have issues with friendships, romantic relationships, or family members.*
>
> *Any beliefs of unworthy, undeserving, less than, inadequate, unlovable, stupid, not enough, not good enough, and/or deserving of punishment, will lead to self sabotaging behavior because it becomes a self fulfilling prophecy (you need to be right because at a subconscious level you believe these things about*

> *yourself). Behavior is just a symptom. It is either a symptom of nourishing beliefs or detrimental beliefs.*

What are you afraid of?

> *I encourage you to invite your fear in and just have a conversation with it. Let it tell you all the things that you fear or are scared of.*

How many of your fears are imminent? (coming right toward you or happening right now)

> *Hint: you would probably not be sitting and writing this right now if there were any. The point here is that you are safe right now. Let that acknowledgement of safety in right now.*

Which of your fears are based in the past?

Which of your past fears are you projecting into the future, causing worry and anxiety?

Which of your fears are anticipatory, not based on a past event?

Remember: you are constructing these, stop. You are causing yourself undo stress, worry, and anxiety.

> *Note: If you have a premonition or gut feeling of something, the only thing you can do is accept it and do your best to plan wisely for it, prepare your heart, mind, and anything physical and then move on knowing you've done all you can in this moment. You are only in control of the very brief present moment. You only have so much control over your physical world, but you have total control over your internal world, accept that.*

Which of your fears can you do something about right now?

Which of your fears are out of your immediate and actual control?

Which of your fears are for others (people you know and don't know)?

What shame do you carry?

What guilt do you carry?

What grief do you carry?

What pain do you carry?

What burden do you carry?

Are you willing to put what you carry down and sort through it?

> *As you sort through it, imagine you had different bins and bags in which you place things. What can go in the garbage? What needs to be incinerated? What can be recycled and turned into something new and better? (utilize the Bonus Light Process, the processes in the back of The Pursuit of More, the Forgiveness Processes, and Forgetting to Remembering Meditation)*
>
> *Example: I experienced a serious autoimmune issue. I didn't know what I was dealing with for a long time. I was struggling. I dealt with incompetent doctors and spending lots of money in useless places. I was doing my best to*

care for myself, but some of the things I was doing turned out to be counterproductive. When I found out what I was dealing with, I knew the more precise actions to take for my care and well-being. Through this I forgave myself, the doctors, and the process. I set new boundaries for myself and with others. I learned to appreciate the chronic pain, fatigue, frustration, and hopelessness others experience with chronic illness and disease. I also gained more understanding, patience, and grace for myself and others to a depth I may not have understood without this experience. I chose to take all the lessons from my journey and discard the difficult and trying emotions, people, and experiences. I chose to be liberated, free, and in a place of forgiveness and LOVE.

The process of transforming this 'thing' that you carry is the very process of transformation. You no longer carry it around in its current form. You can transform ideas, thoughts, beliefs, behaviors, emotions, experiences, illnesses, and really anything else that doesn't serve you. Once it's transformed, you keep that and what it was before gets discarded or disappears into LOVE. This is what allows you to keep the lessons, learnings, and knowledge from that thing, but it no longer weighs you down in any way. It's like placing the healed memory in a fluffy cloud, if you need it as some later date it will gently flow in and provide words of wisdom for another or be a gentle reminder of what you know you know and don't need to learn again.

Suggested Resources

The Power of TED by David Emerald

Practical Miracles by Arielle Essex

Breaking the Habit of Being Yourself by Dr. Joe Dispenza

Molecules of Emotion by Candace Pert

Choice Point Theory - documentary

The Living Matrix - documentary

Spirituality

I personally believe that there is only LOVE and fear. You live life and operate by either one or the other. This can change moment to moment if you are really out of alignment and/or do not have a deeply personal relationship with something greater than you. Some people call this greater than God, Allah, Buddha, Krishna, Vishnu, YHWH, Christ, Universe, Spirit, Life Source Energy, Life Force Energy, Energy, and more. I think of it as LOVE. For some that believe deeply in science, religion is thrown out and a practice of some sort of spirituality is rarely engaged.

Having a spiritual practice is essential for your over-all well-being. You cannot be the healthiest you without some sort of spiritual engagement or practice. Through science they have shown varying vibrations and associations with these varying vibrations. There are heathy vibrations and unhealthy vibrations. Spiritual practices such as being in and with nature, meditation, connection through prayer, utilizing crystals and sound, all produce healthier vibrations.

If religion is absolutely not an option for you, that's okay. You are the one that gets to decide this for yourself, no one else 'should' decide this for you. You owe nothing of your spirit energy to anyone else—and to adhere to something that is not fulfilling, deeply meaningful, uplifting with LOVE, grace, compassion, inclusion, and nourishment, is to abandon and deny your own soul and spirit.

I've worked with people that have all sorts of varying beliefs, and some that didn't know what to believe or if they even wanted to believe in anything. It is false and detrimental to think that there is no greater energy and that there are no intricate and connected systems of energetic intelligence.

Biology is bigger than you; it's bigger than any of us can wrap our heads around. When a sperm hits that egg, energy is released, and even more energy is consumed in the entire creation process. Nature can create and produce things that we know about and have a hard time measuring or figuring out, let alone all that we have yet to discover.

The universe and space are bigger than you; it's bigger than any of us can wrap our heads around. When atoms are split, light is split, harnessed, or transformed; the energy is in many ways still immeasurable. Trees, plants, and mushrooms all have an interconnected underground energy and intelligence with one another, animals, and even us.

Communication and energy exchange are happening whether you are aware of it or not. There are energies and connections that exist that we can't even begin to wrap our heads around, let alone even begin to measure, and yet, it's all still happening.

I encourage you to be utterly honest with yourself. Stay open and curious. Be skeptical in ways that allow for your truth to unfold and present itself. It's your duty to create this relationship for the sake of your utmost well-being. Nurture and nourish this relationship in ways that feel good, meaningful, and fulfilling to you.

You are not your family. You are not your church. You are not your culture. These things have influenced who you are, yes, but you are not them. You get to decide the role any of these things play in your life and how prominent they are for you.

Questions for Reflection

What are your spiritual or religious beliefs?

Is there any part of you that feels out of alignment with these beliefs?

How do these beliefs serve you?

Do they fulfill you?

Do you have any spiritual or religious practices? Is this something you've wanted to entertain more or in different ways?

What spiritual or religious beliefs do you have that you feel cause you grief, despair, guilt, shame, or the like?

Do you feel like your relationship with what you refer to is a strong and healthy relationship?

Is there any quid pro quo within your belief system?

> *According to a person (even you) or some writing: If you do this, then that will happen. Or, I have to do this or adhere to that in order to be this or be seen as that. Or, if I don't do 'x' then I won't get 'y' or be seen as 'y'. This is not a function of natural or organic action and reaction. This is adhering to an 'if, then' manufactured, artificially.*

Do you have a sense of indebtedness just for being alive? Is there a sense of indebtedness that you feel and maybe can't explain why?

If you don't refer to anything, do you feel like that is a strong and healthy relationship for you? How is it strong and healthy or how is it not strong and healthy?

Have you wondered what else is out there or been curious about other belief systems?

Are you willing to look into other belief systems and theories or study them? You do not need to look into other belief systems to become a part of them, but rather to educate yourself a bit more on the subject.

How personal is your relationship with what you refer to, outside of any teachings, books, or specified practices?

Do you want a more personal relationship with what you refer to — something just for you?

Do you meditate?

Do you know how?

Did you know there are many ways to meditate?

> *Connecting to your breath, navigating, and regulating it, and going within yourself is meditation. Opening your awareness to your thoughts, beliefs, feelings, and emotions with observation versus judgement, is meditation. Being present (not the past, not the future, just right now) is meditation. Meditation is about going within, being silent, and listening as best you can. Prayer is about asking or requesting - it's you speaking and not listening.*

Do you pray, ask for something, or make requests? Who and/or what are you referring to when you do this?

Do you feel a connection to who or what you are referring to when you pray, ask, or request?

Do you spend time in and with nature? (without others around and without music or other 'entertainment')

> *Note: This does not include hunting or fishing. I am referring to uninterrupted time hiking, walking, sitting, swimming, where it's just you and the environment around you.*

What can you do to create your own strengthened experience with the energy that you want to refer to?

What and who do you need to forgive?

I encourage you to explore, pursue and seek what feels deeply meaningful and right for you. Until you feel a strong connection, deep peace, and energy that ignites your very soul, keep practicing, and keep connecting to your breath and to LOVING Light. You may experience glimpses or mere moments of connection, peace, and supportive energy - you're on the right path, keep going.

To have either a sense of entitlement or a sense of indebtedness sets you up for experiencing lacking, without, despair, and left wanting. No matter your beliefs, it is important to know that you are part of a connection of energy, not separate from, not more than and not less than. You are simply an expression of energy as it is within your perception. You are enough just as you are and others are enough just as they are, and to think any differently causes divide, separateness, segregation, loneliness, and feelings of being lost.

You can be alone and never feel lonely when you connect to your breath, your heart, and connect to the energy that is in and around everything on earth and in space. This energy is real, it's been measured by multiple fields of science, how you choose to relate to it is your unique experience. Why not make it the best experience for you?

Suggested Resources

The Red Book by Sera Beak

I'm Spiritual Dammit by Jenniffer Weigel

The Universe Has Your Back by Gabrielle Bernstein

You Can Heal Your Life by Louise Hay

Pursuits and Goals

Questions for Reflection

Think back to when you were little, what did you dream about doing, becoming, being a part of, having, and experiencing?

What and who drove those dreams, aspirations, and goals if you were to know?

Do those same dreams, aspirations, goals, and pursuits still apply or fit with who you are now?

If any do, what would be accomplished by accomplishing them?

Would you be pleased with yourself?

Would others be pleased with you? Do you need or crave this?

Is it more important for you to be pleased with yourself or for others to be pleased with you? Which brings about a stronger feeling?

> *Feeling pleased with yourself, void of anyone else's input, is the goal. This is where you are experiencing your truest "self" void of a malnourished ego.*

What do you want more of in your life? List all you can think of: people, money, things, emotions, thoughts, laughter, peace, muscles, etc.

Having more ___ (pull from your list) ____, will benefit and improve your life in the following ways (making life better): _____

_____

Answer using the words me/my.

Having more of ___ (pull from your list) ____, will possibly burden, tie you down, stress you out, and/or 'bury' you in the following ways:_____

_____

Answer using the words me/my.

Do you have a current plan for obtaining and/or attaining these things?

If you do have a plan, have you implemented it?

Is it working?

Does it feel good?

Are any of the things you want a desire for you and your own true fulfillment? Or are they a desire because of something or someone else? Do you want these things because of a desire to compete, to fill a void, to feel important, to be accepted/acceptable, to prove something, to take something away from someone else, or to control something/someone?

In what parts of your life do you know you are contorting and shapeshifting? It may just feel like you're contorting and shapeshifting.

> *Go within, what were you unaware of (until now) that you have been inauthentically doing or saying to be accepted, fit in, not stick out, be liked, be loved, and/or to belong?*

Is there anyone or more than one person that you contort and shape-shift for specifically, and not for the sake of you, but for the sake of them?

Are you aware of any behaviors of yours that are out of alignment with what you believe?

> *You believe ___x___ and yet you do ___y___. [**Or**] You have to will yourself with everything you've got to not do ___y___. This is internal conflict at its finest. This is where detrimental and outdated beliefs are getting in your way, sabotaging, and holding you back.*

What do you dream about doing, becoming, being a part of, having, and experiencing?

What all do you want to pursue and/or accomplish?

Do you feel you are worthy and deserving of accomplishing what you really want?

How do you know it's time to take action?

Do you have issues/problems with taking action?

How many people do you consult before making a decision and/or taking action?

> *This refers specifically to decisions you are making for yourself, not for jobs, a family, or bigger group.*

Do you feel you can rely only on yourself to make a decision or take action?

> *This refers specifically to decisions you are making for yourself, not for jobs, a family, or bigger group.*

Is there anyone or anything that motivates you but is not inspiring?

> *Inspiration comes from your soul being sparked by something that speaks to your deep truth and knowing. Inspiration fills you and provides wonderful energy and even fuel for a potential process of embarking on something. Motivation is external - sparked by something you want to obtain that you do not currently have/possess. Money can be a motivator but is not necessarily inspiring. You can be motivated by wanting to avoid pain. You can be motivated by obtaining a specific title. Your parents can motivate you and also not be inspiring. You can be motivated positively and negatively by something you want to happen or something you want to avoid.*

Who and what do you find inspiring?

When and where do you feel most inspired and motivated?

What do you want to do every day?

What do you only want to do sometimes?

What do you never want to do again?

What do you want to do by the end of your life, your legacy, if you will?

Where do you want to live and how do you want to live? (stay in one place, move year to year, or travel around as you wish with a home base or no home base)

How much of what you've already answered is a reality for you right now?

What and/or who is holding you back or keeping you from starting, continuing, or completing your pursuits and/or goals? Some answers may come easily to your mind and other might come up and surprise you, either way you know, allow yourself to access that knowing.

Who and what are dictating your life decisions and life directions?

Were you ever told you can't have something in life or be something in life because of ___x___?

What about this thing or person is so powerful? It must be powerful because it's keeping you from creating, being, and doing.

When did you give/allow that thing or person so much power?

What do you need to do in order to reclaim that misdirected energy?

> *Hint: You'll find the answers within yourself and both The Pursuit of Forgiveness 2.0 and The Pursuit of More can help you awaken to what you need.*

We have many pursuits and only one journey. The journey lies within the pursuit. Obtaining information, gaining knowledge, and apply both as practices in your life will instill wisdom and help you experience clarity. Choosing a pursuit is imperative, finishing it is not. Sometimes in the middle of the pursuit is where you get the 'gold nugget' and that was the whole point for that particular pursuit. Collect the nuggets and calibrate from there. You will know when the pursuit has reached its final destination. The final destination of any pursuit is the knowing that you got exactly what you needed from it and there is no desire to keep going, not because you feel stuck, overwhelmed, or the like, but because you feel accomplished and a natural finality. You may pivot in that pursuit or you may just experience the fulfillment and move on to the next.

> *Example: You set a goal to do an Ironman Race. You start your pursuit in eventually completing an Ironman Race. You start the training and doing what you need to get in shape. You carve out the time you need, you eat healthier, and you set better boundaries in order to hone your focus and experience less distraction. You run smaller marathons. You run some bigger marathons. It's getting closer to the Ironman and you feel like it's no longer something you need to accomplish. What*

completing this race meant when you first started out is not what it's feeling like it means anymore. You have many other marathons you've completed to this point and you continue to set better time finishes at each race. It's just fun now and you've continued to experience more joy and freedom throughout the entire process. The pursuit led you to enjoying other activities, establishing new relationships, and helping you grow in other areas of your life.

In setting the goal and pursuing an Ironman Race, you reclaimed your time, you reclaimed your health, you established a new routine, you feel accomplished, satisfied, fulfilled, and determined in continuing the new habits you've established. It was never really about the Ironman, it was about reclaiming your life, your way. The Ironman is not the cherry on the sundae that you consume and then is done with, it was the rainbow that led you to a different way of life that has no finish line. Because of this pursuit you've set other goals, reshaped old goals, and allowed yourself to know that the process itself is what made the goal complete.

Setting goals and pursuing them is about tending to your well-being so that you can show up as the best version of yourself for yourself—to live a life that feels good and is filled with more joy, happiness, fulfillment, and LOVE. This is how you contribute to your greater good and to the collective greater good. The less people are consumed by or with other people, the more energy and attention they have to focus on making sure they are being their best self and others can focus on being their best self. Then, we all just get to share our best selves with others.

Being your best self and sharing your best self requires forgiving yourself and forgiving others. There is never a need to hold a grudge and no goodness or prosperity ever comes from holding a grudge. Your best self requires you to LOVE yourself wholly and completely as you are. It requires that you fall deeply in LOVE with yourself. This is the only way to continue to grow, evolve, and continue to heal. This is the only way to get through every trial, tribulation, frustration, and challenge. This is how you navigate it all more easily, more peacefully, and in a more efficient and timely manner.

Remember to always show up as YOU, no matter the situation. When you deny being yourself you will find yourself surrounded by people and things you don't really like or want around—you can even find yourself in situations and places that don't feel good, represent you, or feed and nourish you. When you show up courageously as yourself, for yourself, you automatically set the energy and intention for what you will allow into your life—this goes for career and any relationship. By being YOU, always, you will create the most beneficial surroundings and people. This is how you create your life by design. Show up as YOU, know how dynamic and incredible you are - honor, nourish, and take care of this being. You do this by just being you: confidently, lovingly, calmly, boldly, YOU! Once you have fully accepted yourself no one can deny you of who you are and what you can accomplish. Never bend to or for another, and never allow another to bend to or for you.

You will know when you are not authentically and congruently being you and are in fact creating your life by design because you will find yourself feeling depleted, left wanting, searching, unhappy, unfulfilled, and wandering mentally, emotionally, and physically with constant anticipation.

Bring yourself back to alignment and authenticity by establishing a meditative practice, working with LOVING Light, spending quality time with yourself, and quality time in and with nature. Stay open and curious to your thoughts, beliefs, behaviors, and intentions. Dig in and do the work when needed. Life is not static, it's dynamic. Due to the dynamic nature of life, you will always have some work to do, but it will seem less daunting when you know how to do it and allow yourself to do it. You will move through the difficult times with more ease and LOVE. You will gain even deeper insights, experience more gratitude, and the difficult stuff will be experienced less often.

So, boldly and brilliantly BE YOU! Allow your personality with all the beauty and quirks to shine brightly. Know what is okay in your life and what is not. Be your own compass that is consistently in alignment with your internal stars.

Suggested Resources

Screw It Let's Do It by Richard Branson

Finding My Virginity by Richard Branson

You Are A Badass by Jen Sincero

Dare to Lead by Brene Brown

Presence by Amy Cuddy

Create Your New Narrative
Express Your Soul

Describe your ideal self, living your ideal life. Who and what are in it? How do you feel, think, and behave? Where do you live? What do you do for a career, hobbies, fun, etc.? What permissions do you give yourself once and for all?

> *Channel Bob Ross here... 'Paint' and create your life with every wonderful detail you can imagine. Take this document and place it somewhere safe and special. Somewhere you can read it as often as you want and need. Let this be your driving force to continuously create the life of your soul's wishes.*

Write your very own permission slip, similar to the one in the back of *The Pursuit of More*. Place it in your office, room, wherever you need it so that it can continue to inspire you. Rewrite as needed.

Remember that you are worthy and deserving of LOVE. You are worthy and deserving of good things, good people, healthy relationships, good feelings, and of respect, honor, and dignity. You are enough; allow your soul to shine and remind you of this.

Resources

Books

- *Biology of Belief* by Bruce Lipton, PhD
- *The Honeymoon Effect* by Bruce Lipton, PhD
- *Molecules of Emotion* by Candace Pert
- *The True Power of Water* by Masaru Emoto
- *You Can Heal Your Life* by Louise Hay
- *The Power of TED* by David Emerald
- *Practical Miracles* by Arielle Essex
- *You are a Badass* by Jen Sincero
- *Love, Medicine, & Miracles* by Bernie Siegel, MD
- *Screw It, Let's Do It* by Sir Richard Branson
- *The Virgin Way* by Sir Richard Branson
- *The Pursuit of Forgiveness 2.0: Unlocking Pragmatic Forgiveness* by Melissa Reese
- *The Pursuit of More* by Melissa Reese
- *Presence* by Amy Cuddy
- *The Anatomy of Calling* by Lissa Rankin
- *Mind Over Medicine* by Lissa Rankin
- *The Universe Has Your Back* by Gabrielle Bernstein
- *Finding Your Way In a Wild New World* by Martha Beck
- *The Untethered Soul* by Michael A. Singer
- *Dare to Lead: Brave Work. Tough Conversations. Whole Hearts.* by Brene Brown
- *Braving the Wilderness* by Brene Brown
- *Big Magic: Creative Living Beyond Fear* by Elizabeth Gilbert

- *Tiny Beautiful Things: Advice on Love and Life from Dear Sugar* by Cheryl Strayed
- *Breaking the Habit of Being Yourself* by Dr. Joe Dispenza
- *Becoming Supernatural* by Dr. Joe Dispenza
- *The Mastery of Self* by Don Miguel Ruiz Jr.
- *The Five Levels of Attachment* by Don Miguel Ruiz Jr.
- *The Four Agreements by* Don Miguel Ruiz
- *The Fifth Agreement* by Don Miguel Ruiz
- *The Mastery of Love: A Practical Gide to the Art of Relationship* by Don Miguel Ruiz

Instagram Profiles

@thepursuitguru (Melissa Reese)

@yung_pueblo (Yung Pueblo)

@morganharpernichols (MHN: Morgan Harper Nichols)

@drjoedispenza (Dr. Joe Dispenza)

@_guidley_ (Guidley)

@Steven (Steven Bartlett)

@the.holistic.psychologist (Dr. Nicole LePera)

@anitamoorjani (Anita Moorjani)

@rythmia (Rythmia)

@robriccardo (Rob Riccardo)

@celebrateyourlifeevents (Celebrate Your Life Events)

@wearegaia (Gaia)

@sadhguru (Sadhguru)

Television Shows & Documentaries

Gaia TV (Subscribe and get access to shows and documentaries. You will find information on healing, health, food, meditation, yoga, and much more.)

What the Bleep Do We Know?

The Cure Is

Choice Point Theory

The Living Matrix

Heal Documentary

www.ingramcontent.com/pod-product-compliance
Lightning Source LLC
Chambersburg PA
CBHW071322080526
44587CB00018B/3316